I WANT TO KNOW

Are Dragons Real?

Portia Summers and
Dana Meachen Rau

Enslow Publishing
101 W. 23rd Street
Suite 240
New York, NY 10011
USA
enslow.com

Published in 2017 by Enslow Publishing, LLC
101 W 23rd St. Suite 240 New York, NY 10011

Library of Congress Cataloging-in-Publication Data

Names: Summers, Portia, author.
Title: Are dragons real? / Portia Summers and Dana Meachen Rau.
Description: New York : Enslow Publishing, 2017. | Series: I want to know | Includes bibliographical references and index.
Identifiers: LCCN 2016024700| ISBN 9780766082342 (library bound) | ISBN 9780766082328 (pbk.) | ISBN 9780766082335 (6-pack)
Subjects: LCSH: Dragons—Juvenile literature.
Classification: LCC GR830.D7 S86 2016 | DDC 398.24/54—dc23
LC record available at https://lccn.loc.gov/2016024700

Printed in China

To Our Readers: We have done our best to make sure all websites in this book were active and appropriate when we went to press. However, the author and the publisher have no control over and assume no liability for the material available on those websites or on any websites they may link to. Any comments or suggestions can be sent by e-mail to customerservice@ enslow.com.

Photo Credits: Cover © iStockphoto.com/mppriv; pp. 3, 9 Kiev.Victor/Shutterstock.com; p. 4 Coneyl Jay/Stone/Getty Images; p. 6 Acme Imagery/SuperStock; p. 7 (top) Luis Santos/ Shutterstock.com; p. 7 (bottom) 45RPM/DigitalVision Vectors/Getty Images; p. 8 John Gress/ Corbis News/Getty Images; p. 11 AF archive/Alamy Stock Photo; p 12 DEA Picture Library/ DeAgostini/Getty Images; p.13 Universal Images Group/Getty Images; p. 15 Philip and Elizabeth De Bay/Corbis Historical/Getty Images; p. 16 Dorling Kindersley/Getty Images; p. 17 kimberrywood/DigitalVision Vectors/Getty Images; p. 18 Imagemore Co, Ltd./Getty Images; p. 19 Ironsv/Shutteerstock.com; p. 20 Moment/Getty Images; p. 21 Mark Garlick/Science Photo Library/Getty Images; p. 22 Kike Calvo/National Geographic Magazines/Getty Images; p. 23 Michael Dunning/Photographer's Choice/Getty Images; p. 25 Australian Scenics/Photolibrary/ Getty Images; p. 26 Ginger Livingston Sanders/Shutterstock.com.

Contents

Chapter 1

As Old As Time

Poets and storytellers all over the world have told tales about dragons. Some of these tales had dragons that were **murderous** and cruel. Others had dragons that were kind and protected humans. Some dragons breathed fire. Others granted wishes and gave gifts.

Show Some Respect!

There are many different types of dragon. They can range in size, abilities, color, and even **temperament**. However, all the legends do agree on one thing: dragons are sensitive and should always be treated with respect.

Here, There, and Everywhere

In **cultures** all over the world, people recorded their history. They included myths in their writings. This helped to spread these stories. Many people believed they were true. Some of the earliest stories about dragons came from Ancient Babylon and Egypt. Egyptians believed that their sun god, Ra, defeated a dragon-like beast each night and rose again each day. In Babylon, Tiamat [TYAH-maht] was a dragon goddess of salt water. She gave birth to all of the gods. Sirrush is another Babylonian dragon-creature with a scaly dragon's body, the legs of a lion, a

The famous Ishtar gate in ancient Babylon (modern-day Iraq) depicted many mythical creatures, including dragons.

long neck and tail, and an eagle's **talons**. This creature is on the famous Ishtar Gate, which protected the city of Babylon for thousands of years.

Imagine That!

In European tradition (above), dragons are most often considered dangerous. In Chinese tradition (left), dragons are considered lucky.

In Ancient Greece, Homer talked about dragons in his famous **epic** *The Illiad.* The celebrated king Agamemnon is described as wearing a blue dragon on his sword belt. In fact the word "dragon" comes from the Greek word *draconata*, [dra-CON-ah-tah] which means "to watch."

In the Americas, Quetzalcoatl [KET-sa-koat-el] (below) was the god of wind and wisdom. This giant feathered serpent was worshipped all over Central America.

Chapter 2

Western Dragons

The dragons of European stories were massive creatures with snake-like or **reptilian** bodies. Some had two legs, and others had four. Some had wings, and some could breathe fire. They killed with their sharp talons and teeth. Most dragons only had one head. But the Greek dragon Typhon [TAHY-fon] had a hundred!

Pliny the Elder, who wrote the first book about animals of the world, said that dragons could strangle and elephant with their tails. **Naturalists** of the time thought that dragons were related to snakes.

Guardians of Gold

In European stories, dragons watched over great treasures. Deep in caves, high in mountains, or at the bottom of the ocean they guarded over piles of gold and gemstones. In early stories they rarely attacked humans (unless they were really hungry!). But as time went on, the stories told more and more of dangerous beasts that would happily snack on a person or a whole field of sheep.

Dragon Slayers

Many European myths tell of dragon **slayers**. These brave heroes won treasure, wisdom, or the love of a princess when they defeated a dragon. One of the most famous stories

Most Famous Dragons

Authors and filmmakers have continued to tell stories about dragons. J.R.R. Tolkien (*The Lord of the Rings*), J. K. Rowling (*Harry Potter*), and George R.R. Martin (*A Song of Ice and Fire*) have all used dragons in their stories. But some dragons are more famous than others. Here are a few iconic dragons and where you can find them:

- Falkor, *The Never Ending Story* (1984)
- Saphira, *Eragon*
- Mushu, *Mulan* (1998, below)
- Smaug, *The Hobbit*
- Elliot, *Pete's Dragon* (1977, 2016)

- "Puff the Magic Dragon"
- Godzilla
- Haku, *Spirited Away* (2001)
- Maleficent, *Sleeping Beauty* (1959)
- Toothless, *How to Train Your Dragon* (2010)

about a dragon slayer is that of Staint George (below). According to the legend, there was a town that was being terrorized by a dragon. In order to keep the dragon from destroying the town, they gave it two sheep every day. When the townspeople ran out of sheep, they began feeding their children to the dragon. The children were chosen at random. Finally, the king's daughter was chosen. He promised to give away all his money if she would be spared.

Saint George came along just as the princess was about to be given to the dragon. He made the **sign of the cross** and charged the dragon. He killed it with his **lance**. In thanks, the townspeople **converted** to Christianity, and George later became a saint. The English still celebrate St. George on his holiday of April 23.

Basiliscus, Basilisck.

Imagine That!

According to European legends, there are many creatures related to dragons. Giant snakes, hydras, gargoyles, wyvern, and basilisks were all related to dragons.

Another famous dragon slayer is Beowulf. An epic was written about Beowulf and his adventures. As a young man, he defeated a monster called Grendel. As an old man, he was king of a land called Geat. In this kingdom, a dragon guarded the graves of kings, buried with their treasure. One day, a thief stole some of the dragon's treasure, and the dragon became very angry. It set fire to many villages. Beowulf found the dragon and killed it, but he was hurt in the battle. He died and was buried with the dragon's treasure.

In many European legends, dragons guard vast amounts of treasures, and breathe fire at anyone who comes near it.

Chapter 3

Eastern Dragons

In Asian cultures, dragons are very important. Stories about dragons have come from Japan, India, Korea, Persia, and other cultures. The Chinese are especially fond of dragon stories. Unlike dragons in European myths, the dragons in Chinese tales are not cruel and evil. They are friends to people and are often helpful.

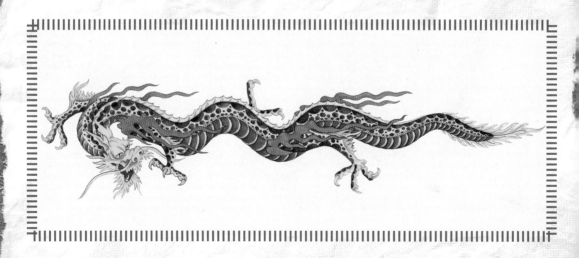

A Symbol of Power

The Chinese thought that dragons had the bodies of snakes, four legs, and a long face with whiskers. The came in different colors and could change their size. They could be tiny enough to fit in your hand or big enough to fill the sky. They could even make themselves invisible. Some Chinese dragons could grant wishes.

Imagine That!

The dragon is one of the signs of the Chinese **zodiac**. A person born under this sign has the qualities that make a good leader and will live a long life.

鼠　牛　虎　兔

龙　蛇　马　羊

猴　鸡　狗　猪

Chinese dragons (right) were associated with power, strength, and good luck, and were often **symbols** for important people like emperors. Chinese dragons were also closely connected to water. According to myth, dragon kings lived in rivers and lakes. They had palaces deep under the water where they kept their treasures. They guarded a large, glowing pearl that they carried in their jaws or chins.

The Chinese also believed dragons controlled the weather. Lightning came from their eyes. They made wind when they flew. The clouds came from dragon's breath. When there was a storm or a flood, people thought the dragons were unhappy. They made **offerings** to the dragons. They wrote prayers on slips of paper and tossed them in a river. They also offered flowers or special stones.

Yin and Yang

The Chinese philosophy of yin and yang is very important to their culture. This idea is all about balance and harmony. The yin represents water, coolness, darkness, gentleness, grace, and rest. The phoenix stands for the yin. The yang represents fire, heat, light, action, strength, and power. The dragon stands for the yang.

Years of Dragons

Today, the dragon is still an important part of Chinese culture. Dragons decorate many rooftops and gardens. The Dragon Boat festival is held every year. The Dragon Dance (below) is performed at Chinese New Year, where they hold up a long colorful dragon puppet made of silk, paper, and bamboo. Long ago, the Chinese did the dragon dance to bring rain for their crops. Today, this dance brings good luck.

Chapter 4

Real-Life Dragons

Ancient peoples thought dragons were real. They prayed to them, feared them, and even sent them offerings. They saw dragons everywhere: in oceans, mountains, and in the clouds. When they found large bones buried in the ground, they thought that these bones were from

Underwater Dragons

The leafy sea dragon is an underwater animal that is related to the seahorse. These creatures look like leaves and have spiny bodies. They live in the waters near Australia.

dragons. Today, we know those large bones are from dinosaurs and other **prehistoric** animals. But it is easy to see how somone that knows nothing of dinosaurs would mistake their fossils for those of dragons.

The Komodo dragon is a real life dragon! These giant lizards are known to have a particularly nasty attitude.

Nerve-racking Reptiles

There are also large species of lizards that seem like dragons. In fact, some myths may be based on large snakes, crocodiles, or lizards. The Gila monster has a heavy, scaly body and drools a lot. When this lizard bites, he clamps down and doesn't let go. The bearded dragon is a gentle lizard that is often kept as a family pet.

The komodo dragon is huge lizard. It can grow up to 200 pounds and has massive claws and teeth. They will eat almost anything—even bones! And their **saliva** is poisonous. Thankfully, they only live in the wild in Indonesia.

Lurking Lizards

Another reptile that might have inspired the dragon myth is the crocodile or alligator. These creatures live both on land and in the water, and have massive mouths

Imagine That!

The thorny devil looks terrifying, but it is too small to harm humans.

What's that in that cave? Is it a reflection? Or is a dragon watching to make sure you don't steal his treasure?

full of razor-sharp teeth. They are exceptionally strong, and will eat anything they can. Their long tails and scaly bodies could easily be mistaken for a dragon.

Today, most people don't believe in dragons, since no one has seen one. But that may just be because dragons are hiding out in places we humans can't go.

Words to Know

culture The ideas, arts, tools, and ways of life of a certain group of people.

epic A long poem that tells the deeds and adventures of a hero.

lance A long weapon made of wood or metal designed to be used by a horseman.

murderous Dangerously violent and capable of killing someone.

myth A story people tell to explain the past or describe unbelievable creatures.

naturalist An expert who studies plants and animals.

offering A gift made to make a person or creature happy.

prehistoric From a time before history.

reptilian Having the characteristics of a reptile.

saliva A liquid that comes from the mouth that aids in digestion.

sign of the cross A movement made by Christians in prayer.

slayer A person who kills others in battle.

symbol Something that stands for something else.

talons The sharp claws of some birds.

temperament Behavior.

zodiac A belt of stars or planets in the heavens that has a certain position in the sky.

Further Reading

Books:

DK Publishing, *Children's Book of Mythical Beasts and Magical Monsters*. New York, NY: Penguin Random House, 2011.

McCall, Gerrie and Chris McNab. *Mythical Monsters Legendary, Fearsome Creatures*. New York, NY: Scholastic. 2011.

Rimes, Raleigh. *Dinsosaurology*. Somerville, MA: Candlewick Press, 2013.

Scamander, Newt. *Fantastic Beasts and Where to Find Them* (Harry Potter). New York, NY: Arthur A. Levine Books, 2015.

Websites:

American Museum of Natural History

www.amnh.org/exhibitions/mythic-creatures/dragons-creatures-of-power

Learn more about dragons from across the world.

San Diego Zoo

kids.sandiegozoo.org/animals/reptiles/komodo-dragon

Read more about the komodo dragon.

Surprise Ride

www.surpriseride.com/16-fun-facts-dragons/

Learn more facts about dragons.

Index